Journey Out of SAD:

Banish the Seasonal Blues NOW!

Victoria C. Leo

ISBN: 978-1-4583-4689-6

Disclaimer: This book is not intended to contradict or to be an alternative to licensed medical care for those with a medical problem. The author is a health coach. She is NOT diagnosing you or dispensing medical advice. It is especially important that you not change or decrease medications without consulting a licensed medical practitioner.

List of Illustrations:

Dedication

Elizabeth Jane Pearson

Ann Jacobs Baird

& Rick W. Baird

In grateful thanks to the universe for the life of my dear adoptive mom, Elizabeth Jane Pearson, who dedicated herself to peace in the world and love for her kids. Her body left this earth on September 30. 2010 but her spirit had departed years earlier. Alzheimer's Dementia destroys the brain of wonderful, vibrant people. We need a cure.

All that I am or ever hope to be, I owe to my angel mother. [Abe Lincoln]

Can one person be blessed twice? Yes, she can. Meeting the love of my life also brought me to the most loving, generous and open-hearted mother-in-law in the world, Ann Baird. Every day I spend with her is a precious gift in my life. She opened her arms wide and gathered me in. I know she will never let me go.

And in grateful thanks to that same universe for bringing me the person I waited half a century for. *"One man in a thousand, Solomon says/Will stick more closely than a brother./But the Thousandth Man will stand by your side/To the foot of the gallows – and beyond." (Rudyard Kipling).*

Some of the conscious and unconscious reasons why we pick our life partners don't bear close examination. This one does. I've always been a Thousandth Man, fiercely loyal and honorable. Now I have a partner and husband who matches my values. We have each other's backs in the vicissitudes of life. We have our joys quadrupled. There is nothing on Earth more important, valuable or humbling than to have an emotional home base where love flows freely and the heart is open.

Why This Book?

I have always been cranky, "down" and lethargic during long patches of dark and dreary weather, for as long as I can remember, way back to childhood. I did love looking out on a scene of blazing sunshine. If the temps got over 90F with high humidity, I just went inside a nice cool building and let the light in. The cobalt blue skies that erupt into view on a clear day give the time from sunrise to sunset an energy and a joy that I am only aware of because I know how debilitating days of darkness are. At night, I have looked up at the sky and felt the same satisfied transcendence of limitless vista. Along the road from childhood to almost-seniorhood, I have lived in upstate and downstate New York, in North Carolina, Arizona, California, Oregon and Washington, along with short stints in New Zealand, Moscow, Russia, Sydney, Australia and a great damp, foggy island with an incredible Botanical Garden that still echoes with the spirit of Sir Joseph Banks. On several cross-country trips, I have visited most of the 50 US states, including the two non-contiguous ones. No matter where I have been on Earth, weeks of continuous cloudy skies have had the same effect on me.

For my first two decades of adulthood, I had more serious health problems to concern me. It is only in my last two decades of adulthood that I have had enough education in biology and psychology, and time for concentrated study, to not only understand my problem but to create effective cures for it. As I did so, I learned about people with the opposite problem, that is, depression when light levels last too long.

Knowledge has to come from education as well as experience, I believe. My journey started with an MA in Biological Anthropology, which gave me a strong foundation in human biology, including the biology of depression. I teach Anatomy and Physiology at the college level. I also collected most of the credits for a second MA in Psychology and Counseling, and I hold a Life Coach credential. I am a Clinical Hypnotherapist. This education in the psych side of depression has been invaluable. I explored Reiki energy healing by taking on a three year training program culminating in certification as a Usui Reiki Master/Teacher. I have been teaching and practicing energy healing for almost thirteen years. My company, Soar With the Eagles, offers customized treatment and coaching on a wide variety of health issues, including seasonal depression.

This book is my personal gift to the world of seasonal sufferers, composed of practical, tested ideas from my own archives of self and clients, as well as the best advice I have culled from reading medical and nursing journals. As always, you need to make your own careful decisions, in consultation with a licensed medical professional.

Table of Contents

Chapter 1

What is SAD?

What is SAD?

Seasonal Affective Disorder is a form of temporary depression associated with a particular season of the year. For some people, this depression occurs when the light levels are high and the daylight streams for more than twelve hours a day. This is called SAD, Summer Variety. For most people, the season of depression is the season of dark. They have SAD, Winter Variety. What constitutes winter varies with location. In the San Francisco Bay Area, where I lived for 25 years, we had three months of mostly-grey skies during December-February. By March, partly-sunny days sprinkled the calendar. It usually wasn't socked-in in November. In central and eastern North Carolina, where I lived for five years, the winter brought cloudy skies with intermittent bright days even in mid-winter. Now I live in an eastern Puget Sound city, where people will quote the annual rainfall statistics defensively, while conclusively and triumphantly announcing that the idea that it rains all the time in Seattle is pure fiction. I gently point out to them that, to the average person, a day composed of the drizzle that doesn't add up to any appreciable rainfall still adds up to a Really Awful Day. Lack of measureable accumulation does not change the dark overcast composition of the climate in this part of the world, which lasts almost continuously for at least nine months. For a winter SAD sufferer, that is about eight months too long!

A normal spring in my town has intermittent partly-sunny days starting in May, and June still includes quite a bit of squally weather. In 2010, spring in my town was indistinguishable from winter, except that it was about ten degrees warmer. Big fat soggy deal. Summer makes us biochemically well again, and fall is still clear most days. In a bad year, like 2010, when summer consisted of two weeks of sunshine and an occasional half-day of partly-cloudy, the intermittent light was not able to keep symptoms at bay.

Seasonal Affective Disorder, Winter Variety [SAD-W], is a potential problem for people with a genetic susceptibility to it, all through the northern tier of the USA and all of Canada. Most of this book is focused on Winter SAD, with a special chapter devoted to Summer SAD, because SAD-W accounts for the bulk of the sufferers. Summer variety [SAD-S] is a factor in the southern tier of US states, especially Texas, Florida and the Southwest desert areas, including southern California. It is also a problem for people in Alaska and the northern provinces and territories of Canada, where sufferers have to deal with up to 23 hours of light every day during the summer. In June, Anchorage experiences a 45-minute twilight as its only relief from blinding light. I loved it. SAD-S sufferers were experiencing deep depression.

It is likely that the long dark of western Washington harms more than the mental health of SAD-W sufferers. Strong evidence suggests that a lack of light during childhood development is a contributing factor in the high incidence of multiple sclerosis [MS] in this area. In addition, many human neural and metabolic processes assume that there will be at least nine months of light per year and go haywire without it. We will explore the other conditions that can contribute to seasonal energy slumps and the rest of the symptoms, over the course of this book.

SAD-W is an equal-opportunity problem, affecting all ethnicities and both sexes. Or maybe not. Do doctors take SAD seriously in dark-skinned people? They should, right? Dark skinned people in high latitudes where light is limited are at risk for rickets and osteomalacia unless they take Vitamin D3 supplements and get plenty of calcium, since their melanin is blocking the UV that would otherwise turn cholesterol-D into a Vitamin D3 precursor. So lack of light already causes dark-skinned people one medical problem. The lack of light creates SAD through a mechanism other than the skin, however. To prevent SAD, you need at least 15 minutes of sunlight that gets into your eyes, and is transmitted to your pineal gland and other brain structures. The exact neurology is way too complicated to get into. The key point is that your eyes need to get the light. That's why the cures for the most severe cases involve light in your eyes. We have no reason to suppose that dark-skinned people have less ability to absorb light into their eyes, but the fact that they have an evolutionary adaptation to high light levels in their skin might lead us to expect other genes that are expecting high light levels. That is an extremely long-winded way of saying that if you have dark skin, be particularly vigilant about any downward mood and energy swing in the winter, and have a serious talk with your doctor or try some of the cures here and see if you start feeling better.

SAD & Kids

In some people SAD-W shows up in childhood. Getting kicked outside to play was a trial to me as a book-loving, quiet and thoughtful child, but it is probably why SAD did not show up until I was too old for the "go outside and play" gambit. Children who spend too much time indoors with video games are probably not faring as well as my Boomer generation did, but I have not found studies on this question. Kids with SAD-S are particularly misunderstood, I think. Here it is, the good old summertime. In the crazy world of the USA, that means three months without school. It is also the season of constant assumptions that you are dying to get outside in the sun and play. But you get depressed every summer. Do parents notice the seasonality or do they immediately rush for the anti-depressant bottle? As a professional purveyor of psych, I can say this: never assume something is psychological until you have thoroughly researched and tested for the biochemical.

The Dangers of Ideology

In this and in any other health care decision, don't let ideology do your thinking for you. I can't tell you how many people come to me with pre-decisions concerning only using naturopaths, never using naturopaths or always/never doing or not doing other things, including taking medications. There is a bit of wisdom we can all borrow from Buddhism, which says that all ideologies are dangerous. Only wisdom is golden, and wisdom does not exist in the world of pre-existing ideas.

How do I know it's SAD?

Most medical professionals can recognize a likely case of SAD, and distinguish it from more comprehensive depression, but – people make mistakes, people are rushed or stressed and sometimes we fail to tell our doc the whole story. It's a good idea to become knowledgeable so you can ask the right questions and help guide your treatment.

What could be compounding SAD, confusing itself with SAD or otherwise bedeviling you and your medical professional?

There are a number of conditions that can lead to symptoms that mimic SAD. These tend to come on gradually, so you may be asking "How could I confuse them with seasonal blues?" The fact that they come on gradually may not be apparent. How the human mind works [I'm going to my psych side now] is that something reaches a threshold and you suddenly become aware of it. Do you then go back in your memory and realize that you have been experiencing that something in increasing increments for six months or six years? Not always.

- **You could have hypothyroidism**. When you thyroid stops producing enough thyroid hormone, your basal metabolism slows down. You gain weight. You are lethargic and feel depressed. Especially if you are over 45, test this.

- **You could be experiencing perimenopause[women] or andropause [men].** When your sex hormones decline, so does your mood, until your body adjusts to the new lower levels, which they will do in time.

  I need to digress for a moment on the subject of hormone replacement. If you're a woman, please don't rush out to embrace replacement hormones in the mistaken notion that bioidentical, natural, etc. will not increase your cancer risk. I know Suzanne Somers has made millions of dollars from telling us that we can live forever and look 25 while we do it, but you're too smart to take medical advice from that completely unqualified source. HRT of any kind will increase your cancer risk AND your risk of cardiovascular disease. The biochemical reality is that menopause is normal and natural. Herbal supplements like Black Cohosh are well studied and you can take goodly amounts of it and feel better. There is a life after the hot flashes subside, sister; just hang on until they do. This advice holds for men as well. If you take testosterone supplements, you are increasing testicular and prostate cancer risk, as well as cardiovascular risk. You also risk feminizing yourself. Yes, you read that right. If you overdose on testosterone, the excess will be turned into various estrogens. You may think that your 25-year old levels are "normal," but your body considers them an overdose; it knows how old you are. The sex hormones are chemically very similar. Your body will try to protect itself from your mistakes by transforming what it doesn't need. Breasts don't improve your physique, dude.

  I am addressing this to you, rather than your doctor, because psych studies show that it is primarily patient pressure on doctors that leads to ill-advised HRT and testosterone prescriptions. **Don't pressure your doctor on this one**. If you have an otherwise excellent physician who jumps straight to HRT, telling you that you can just stay on it for a few years and it'll be OK, do two things: 1) **spend at least 6 months faithfully and seriously**

exploring every single alternative and reciting the mantra "There is no Fountain of Youth" for fifteen minutes, six times/day, and if you can honestly say that you are in extreme distress and have given the alternatives a solid try then 2) **go on HRT and then get off it on the day that you pass the two year point and never, ever go back, no matter what**. Unless you think that breast cancer will be less trouble to deal with than hot flashes. As far as the Fuzzy Brain Syndrome is concerned, you just have to live with it until it gets better. When menopause is really over, your brain will stabilize. Make notes, write things down and be resourceful.

- **You could be responding to a situation that re-occurs every winter**. Was there a death or tragedy that occurred in the winter? It's well-known that family holidays like Thanksgiving and Christmas bring many sad memories to the surface for those of us who did not have ideal childhoods. If you have undiagnosed PTSD around events that happened in winter, you could have seasonal depression caused by this psychological factor, not your biochemistry. You could have experienced a sexual assault at this time of year. 25% of women will be assault or abuse victims during their lifetimes, so this is not a trivial possibility. A mental health professional with experience with PTSD is best. Check the Resources appendix.

- **You could have diabetes** or its precursor, metabolic syndrome. When your sugar metabolism is imperfect, you will be prone to down moods. Most people with sugar problems are overweight, don't exercise regularly and eat a diet high in fats and processed foods, but not all sufferers fit this profile. Regardless of whether you have diabetes in your family, make whatever lifestyle changes you need to make to keep fresh veggies in your diet and weight off your midsection. There are resources in the Appendix. You can explore food choices with a nutritionist through your health insurance, for example. Check this possibility with your medical professional.

- **You could have heart disease**. Depression is one of the side effects.

- **You could have year-round low-level depression** that becomes worse in a particular season. Use hypnotherapy, exercise every day, meditate, learn Reiki, use other therapies before you reach for a pill bottle. Low-level depression responds to exercise and meditation as well as it does to medication.

SAD gets worse with age for these and other reasons:

- it's made worse by **stress**. Added responsibilities mean added stressors. The mid-fifties used to be a time of lowered stress as the nest is emptied and the earlier generations are gone. Today, our frail parents need help, which we lovingly provide, but death tends to come at the end of long periods of disability. That's more stress than earlier generations had. The social safety net has been shredded and nearly everyone's retirement savings and real estate wealth went down, not up, in The Great Recession.

- thyroid levels go down, sex hormones decrease, diabetes and heart disease risks go up – there are more **compounding and confusing factors** that get added in

- **traumas** build up: war, assaults, death. You may have to cope with more and more of these as you grow older. You are coping with the lost dreams of your youth, which may peak or be triggered by specific winter or summer holidays. These are all psychology, not biochemistry-related, causes of depression.

- the forms of **social support** that used to sustain you may start to dry up. When we get out of our twenties and thirties, the people around us may get exasperated with us and tell us to pull ourselves together or get over it. They would never be so stupidly brutal with a diabetic, of course. We may not have people around us who know that SAD is a biochemical disease, like diabetes. You can't Think Positive and get rid of diabetes, or SAD, no matter how many times you re-read The Secret.

Since there are so many explanations for why you might be seasonally depressed, it is useful to divide potential causes into two categories:

1. **Situational/cognitive**. If the depression is caused by how you are THINKING about yourself, the world or an event, then you can use cognitive techniques to change how you think. If reading about situational factors in the seasons suggests that there is a cognitive component to your seasonal blues, then it is worthwhile to heal your habitual thought-patterns. Use Take Back Your Lost Heart: A Toolkit for Living With Courage & Caring in the Turbulent 21st Century for ways to work on this on your own or consult a mental health professional. Hypnotherapy and EMDR are valuable for traumas.

2. **Physiological**. If the depression is caused by your physiology, then it must be addressed by changing your physiology. No amount of cognitive therapy or positive thinking will cure a genuine biochemical case of SAD.

This book was created for people who have had a definitive diagnosis, but you can use it if you haven't. Just make sure that you have a medical professional you trust that you can ask questions of, whenever you need to. Nothing in this book is designed to substitute for medical care.

Chapter 2

Easy Cures to Start With -

Which May be Enough for Mild Cases

& Are the Place to Start for Moderate to Severe Cases

When you are thinking about strategies to improve your health, pretend that you are building a house. Decorating the 2nd floor is fun, but the first thing you need to do is build a strong foundation. You lay a level slab or you build the basement. It's not fun, it's not cool and sexy, but it is completely and absolutely essential. That is what this chapter is about. These are the healthy equivalent of laying that foundation. So don't do a slapdash job. Don't do it for a couple of weeks and then quit, because you're "too busy" or it "didn't work." As for busy: Nothing on earth could possibly be more important than pouring your slab or keeping yourself out of life-sapping depression. As for the lack of an instant cure: Things worth getting are worth working at for more than two weeks. Instant transformation only happens in sitcoms.

ith the Easy Three: vitamins/minerals, available light and warmth.

s/Minerals

e 1500 units daily of Vitamin D3, with 1500 units of Calcium and balancing Magnesium if you are in one of the northern states or provinces where light levels are poor. You can get by with 1200 if you have at least 2 full days of sun every week. Make sure you take a good B-complex vitamin, with an extra dose of B-12, because B-12 is good for all kinds of low-energy and depression. If you can afford CoQ10 without sending your babies to bed hungry or giving away the pup, do that as well. L-carnitine is another energy booster. [This is what my wonderful MD recommends. See what your medical provider thinks about these levels.] People like me with diagnosed cases of SAD frequently take 2,000 units, but do stay away from mega-dosing unless you are working with a real medical practitioner; someone making a product pitch is not able to prescribe for you and your unique medical needs. Vitamin D is a fat-soluble molecule, which persists in tissues and can build up to toxic levels.

Available Light

Go out into the natural light whenever it is available, for at least 15 minutes/day. Yes, I know you are working for a taskmaster and you are terrified of the miserable job market. Even so. If you see a break in the clouds and dark, get outside. Grab some file folders and walk purposefully to a nearby building. Find something that needs doing. If all else fails, take a brisk walk around the building. If the President of the USA can walk away from his desk for 15 minutes, what are you doing that will cause the world to implode if you walk around purposefully in the sunshine for the same time period? Seriously? 15 minutes?

Get warm

If you are cold, your body is working overtime to keep your internal body temperature where it needs to be. Your extremities get cold.

Start with the obvious:

➢ **Bundle up.**

[Note to my beloved readers in or from Florida, Texas & California. You do not, in fact, have a constitutional right to wear t-shirts outdoors year round. Glad I could clarify that for you.] Go down to your local high-quality thrift store and buy yourself ten gorgeous sweaters in varied colors. If you pick the right store, and you go on the day when they are having a sale, you could end up with ten sweaters for forty-five bucks plus tax. [Place them from the bag into a warm water wash immediately, then dry them on high heat, to eliminate any chance of a bedbug invasion.]

➢ **Wear socks to keep your feet warm.**

Spend a little extra and get some really nice ones. Get snuggly indoor slippers.

➢ **Buy a heavy, fuzzy bathrobe, preferably in a bright, sunny color.**

I wear tasteful colors in summer and early fall. When the Eternal Clouds roll in, circa October, I pull all my winter clothes out of storage, along with my heavy, bright-orange bathrobe. Tasteful, no. Warm, oh yes. Cheerful? Cowabunga! $3 at Goodwill, on sale. And guys - real men wear red. Psych studies say that people's pupils dilate when they see the color red. This reflects an increase in overall level of physiological arousal. You want your favorite person to increase their level of physiological arousal when they catch sight of you, right? I thought so.

➢ **Raise the temperature in the house.**

I know, I know, your spouse is really Green and will have a fit. Too bad. It's your health at stake. You need to get warm in order to get well. How much does s/he love you? It really is that simple.

Tell him if he really wants to save the world, he can buy his mum compact fluorescents for Mother's Day instead of the roses and chocolates she really wants. See how dedicated he is when it's a matter of the *mater*'s disappointment and disapproval. He can also plan his next vacation exclusively on Amtrak. Every person on one airplane trip puts more greenhouse gases into the upper atmosphere, where they do the most harm, than they would do if they drove their car for a year AND kept their houses at a healthy level. People without SAD can live in cold houses. You can't.

➢ **Take a hot bath, with Epsom salt, every night.** Lavender scent if you can. In addition to warming up your body, the lavender scent will send a relaxation message to your brain; this is cheap aromatherapy. Yes, it uses more water than a shower. It's your health, honey. [Or dude.]

➢ **Visit friends with hot tubs**. They exist. Why do you think I have so many friends? They tell me it's my sparkling personality. Uh-huh.

➢ **If you ever intend to book time at a day spa, do it in mid-winter**. Get services that involve heat and bright light. Sales of pedicures and facials for men are way up. Probably SAD sufferers!

➢ **When you travel, consider motels with saunas**.
The budget chains, like Motel 6 and TraveLodge, have been upgrading their facilities. I visited a Motel 6 outside Dallas that had marble countertops, hardwood floors, a bathroom out of House Beautiful, and cost $39.95. It also had a sauna and hot tub. I wanted to move in permanently.

After the Basic 3, there are four more to consider for mild cases, and as the baseline for more serious cases: **stimulants, movement, social connections and fun**. All these have an effect on your physiology, raising the levels of the chemicals that you need for a positive mood.

Manage Your Levels of Stimulants

No, not the stuff they talk about on cop shows. I'm talking tea and coffee and sodas, oh my. Get yourself detoxed if you have been drinking more than one cup of full-caff every day. Go completely herb tea, no caffeinated sodas either, for at least 30 days. You'll have headaches and other caffeine withdrawal symptoms, but you'll get through it. Do this in the summer.

As cloudy weather gets going, slowly start re-introducing stimulants. Check the weather every day. If it looks like it is going to be a snarly day, make it a full-caff day. If you have detoxed yourself, you'll get buzzed on 8 ounces. No 20-ounce nonsense here! If there are several nasties in a row, alternate decaf or black tea with full-caff. Your goal is to be able to boost your mood and energy level with a small level of caffeine. South American mate is another good choice. It contains a small amount of caffeine, but it seems to be stimulating without causing jittery anxiety.

If you have any medical conditions – like high blood pressure, kidney disease, incontinence, fibrocystic breast disease, bladder disease, diabetes and others – that can be exacerbated by caffeine, for goodness sake, don't have any! Talk to your health care professional about your particular situation.

There is a reason why Starbucks  started in downtown Seattle and the Pacific Northwest boasts three coffee shops and drive-through kiosks on every block. We're self-medicating.

Exercise

Working up a sweat nearly every day is good advice when dealing with any form of "down" emotional state. Movement gets the endorphins generated and improves your overall health. As I explained earlier, low to moderate levels of depression can be alleviated by a daily exercise program.

Ways to Manipulate Your Brain Chemistry, Based on Your Behavior

Do you remember my saying that SAD is a biochemical problem, not a Positive Thinking problem? That's still true. What we are going to explore in this section are some behavioral things that you can do that actually change your brain chemistry.

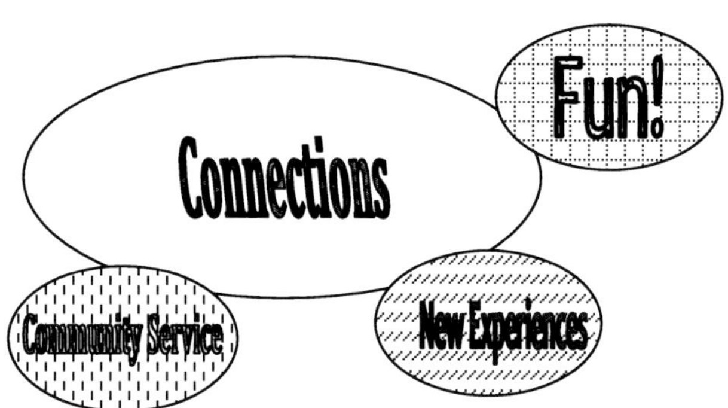

The way I have grouped these "behavioral manipulations" includes three main headings – Fun, New Experiences and Community Service – and one super-heading – Connections. The super heading is there to remind you that the fun, the novelty and the community service will all have their positive effects multiplied if you do them in the context of a supportive social network. People are still getting their PhD's studying how people with rich social networks have better physical health, better mental health, better incomes, better sex lives, write more books [OK, I made that one up].

Let me be really explicit about what I mean. I do NOT mean that introverts like me are doomed to be serial killers and die in a half-collapsed shack, depressed and talking to the ghosts of my ancestors. Introverts, in fact, are over-represented in the annals of the movers and shakers of our species. We just hate parties. No, what I am talking about here is whether you have people to join you in activities some of the time, and whether you have people who you know care about you and will come running with chicken soup if they know you're sick or need help. Most days, you should see someone, talk to someone or do something with someone, and you and the someone should smile or laugh or feel a warm something in your tummy that does not stem from consuming a liquid. Social types [Myers-Briggs E's] have a larger number of acquaintances and chums. Introverts {Myers-Briggs I's] have a smaller number of deep friends. Those nuances don't matter. What matters is that you get connected with other human beings. Animals and plants also feed your soul, but you can't live on that alone. For optimal mental and physical health and happiness, you need to have adult relationships with peers – people you are not responsible for, or have to take care of. You need people that you just enjoy, Friends, in the original meaning of the word, before it became a synonym for "some person I just met."

Having fun increases your brain's serotonin levels, and also boosts other neurotransmitters. The second category – new experiences – requires some explanation. Your brain is an incredible energy-hog. When you are really thinking, you burn up one heck of a lot of glucose. Neurons, therefore, go into idle mode when they are not working. It's how our ancestors were able to grow this big brain without needing to eat 24x7. When you encounter some new stimulus – you see, hear, smell, taste, touch something you have never experienced before – your brain perks up. Your neurons are working and more serotonin is released. You feel happy. Now, there are some new experiences that evoke fear, even terror. In this case, your brain wakes up all right, but not in a good way. Let's just focus on positive or neutral experiences. Of course, if the new environment is a Starbucks you've never been in before, the pleasure hit you get from the new experience is not very strong because there's not much new there. But taking a new class, taking a new hike or trying a new restaurant, faith community or movie will have a measureable impact.

So let's explore these categories!

Have Fun!

It really saddens me to see how many people make a lazy grab for anti-depressants because they "don't have time" to do the things that would make them well without drugs. Let me ask you to be really, really honest with yourself before you conclude that every single unfun thing on your plate is so essential that the police will cart you away to jail for child endangerment if you don't do it. Just for now, read through the list WITHOUT your automatic knee-jerk "I can't" mantra working. Humor me.

As a preliminary: Check through your rusty friendship networks and see what relationships you can resurrect. Warm up the friendships that are intact. **What kinds of things did you used to do? Look through the fun list that follows.** Especially if you used to have some kind of regular commitment, like a bowling league or a weekly pickup basketball game or hiking group, get back in touch.

So what kinds of fun are there to have? Note that many of these are going to fit in the New Experiences category too! Many of them are creative. **Studies of both pain and depression show that engrossing creativity pushes pain away and lightens depression as effectively as medication for many people**. I teach a class called Creative Chakras that shows people how to clear blockages in their energy by engaging in creative activities that exercise one or more of the seven energy centers.

Take a class in an interesting subject that has no career relevance whatsoever. Don't network for work during the class; DO find new friends.	Go to Meetup.com and find a fun group
Learn a new hands-on craft. Learn pottery. Learn glass-blowing. Learn stained glass.	Join a local HAM club. You get the thrill of being helpful in local emergencies and in between the adrenalin rushes you get to hang out with fun people.
Make art. Use colors. Start with detailed coloring books that you find at museums and zoos, or online from Devon and use colored pencils from a craft store. Take a painting class at your local community center, preferably one that teaches quick techniques to get you started creating. Watch a Bob Ross painting DVD from the library or Netflix.	Make a list of local museums and visit one each weekend. The local coupon books have discount tickets.
Get local tour guidebooks from the library. Pick a new place to visit every weekend.	Buy a local coupon book and pick two items weekly.
Learn to make music by taking up an instrument. Your voice is an instrument, too. Join your church choir. Or for less commitment, sing along with your CDs for at least 20 min every day.	Listen to live music. Lots of bookstores and respectable places have live music. Booze, drugs and sleazy attire is not required.
Join a team doing something fun. [Avoid the highly competitive. It's less effective against SAD.]	Visit bookstores that have talks.
Write poetry. Write a memoir of your family. [Don't ask for feedback; don't show it to anyone who might critique. To beat depression, you need bubbling joy. Just do it for yourself.]	Go to a toy store and buy some stuff. Make models- model planes, ships, doll houses. [Things that are absorbing are good. Make sure that you also have things that are social in your life.]
Get involved in an environmental project that involves a minimum of angry emotions and is productive – like building nest boxes for rare birds, counting birds or animals in transects, refurbishing trails, etc.	Create things to give away – crocheted hats in winter; a dog house; a pet bed; a quilt. If you have any carpentry urges, find a non-profit that needs you. Read the local paper to discover groups.
Visit zoos, aquariums, wildlife rehab and animal-related sites.	Find a local contra-dance or ethnic folk dancing group.
Take a class to learn a new language. Make sure it involves other people. Studying alone at home isn't as	Join a book discussion group at your library.

effective.	
Pull out a map of your town or region and make a list of the parks, refuges and other "nature" sites. Get their URls. Visit the ones that sound the most different or the most fun.	Buy tickets to a lesser-known sport and get someone to go with you, either someone who knows a lot and can teach you or someone who knows as little as you, so you can puzzle it out together.
Go to a craft store. Find some paint-your-own holiday ornaments and put some craft paint into your shopping cart. [Men are still manly if they make holiday ornaments. I checked with the Dalai Lama.]	Bring your digital camera somewhere, even the parking lot of your workplace, and snap away. Photography forces you to see the world through new eyes, which wakes up your brain.
Rent, buy or borrow joke tapes. I have the entire Prairie Home Companion joke collection and I listen while I commute under dreary skies.	Start collecting jokes - not the nasty kind. Use this as an excuse to get connected with people at church and in your social network.
Volunteer at your local animal shelter. Dogs need to be socialized. Cats need cuddling. Pick up the poop too. This is a great way to give and receive some love without having the FT care of a pet, or if you have housing that does not permit animals.	If you don't have a pet, consider adopting a friend who will cuddle with you. Cats, rats, guinea pigs – they are all waiting for you at your animal shelter or local rescue group. Dogs will make you get out and interact with other people.
Join a dog-walking group, on Meetup or elsewhere. You don't need your own dog. People will love you forever if you praise their dog or their child.	Attend interesting events at local indy coffeehouses. Find things in your local indy paper. If you've never picked one up, that qualifies as a new thing for this week!
Sign up for CERT or NET and learn how to save your community in an emergency. The classes are interesting and you get to meet nice folks who can become friends.	Join a Meetup or other group that is exploring philosophical topics or includes meditation or yoga. Getting your brain engrossed in philosophical or spiritual ideas raises serotonin levels. Stay away from "angry God" ideas.
Go to a nice modern thrift store. Buy yourself something that makes you smile – clothes, knickknacks, music, books or housewares.	What have you been secretly thinking about but telling yourself that it's too silly, etc?

Pick just one item that you will do this week and write it down here. Getting kids and spouses involved in this fun is definitely allowed! Some of these ideas will be explored in detail in later chapters.

____

Now take a deep breath and go back over the list. Circle, highlight or number them.

If child care burdens are holding you back, keep in mind that our US pioneer ancestors and our Native American ancestors – oh, heck, I have an anthropology degree, everyone in the world – used to have child care co-ops so that we'all could get our work done, have fun and know the kids were running in safe packs under the watchful eye of an adult.

1. Start with other parents. Get your neighbors together. Sally watches all the kids on Monday, Mike watches all the kids on Wednesday and someone's mother, brother or minister watches the kids on Friday. You get one night a week to go to class for something fun, or do your bowling or rumba practice.

2. Try your single friends, relatives and neighbors. Many folks who don't have kids full-time like the energy and creativity and nurturing that an evening with rug rats or school-age kids can bring them. Once a month is good. We have all become aware and sensitized to issues of child abuse, and this is good. Careful is good. Just be reasonable. All of your neighbors and friends are not child molesters.

3. If you have a spouse, give them ownership of their meals and their children at least once/week while you have the fun that you need to stave off your illness. No, it really isn't "complicated." Love is the simplest form of decision-making in existence. Their beloved is ill and s/he needs help. That's not complicated at all.

The other hairy problem, after childcare, is **fear of criticism.** In US culture, we revel in tearing each other down, whereas in other cultures, people are taught to encourage each other. Realize that you have a more or less relentless inner critic whose voice you may be hearing as you go through the list. The message boils down to this: **what if you don't do it well?**

News flash! You're supposed to do it badly the first time you do anything. Call your mum and dad on the phone and ask them how many times you fell down before you learned how to walk on two legs. It's hard to balance! Now you can do it well. I was born with some kind of screw-up in my brain's gross motor coordination area. That's a technical way of saying I can't coordinate big movements very well. Asking me to raise my left arm and move my right leg at the same time is asking for a major mental task. So I could have stayed away from dancing, knowing I was never going to be any good at it. But I didn't intend to give up until I had really tried. So I persisted and guess what? I am the most accomplished, beautiful waltz'er and polka'er you ever saw, and I can do English Country [think a Jane Austen movie], contra, some Latin and a bunch of folk dancing. I had to practice every move about 14 gazillion times before my brain "got" it, but so what**?**

Memorize and practice this mantra:

I don't care what you think of me, why should I?

If you think I'm dumb, a klutz or untalented, what the heck do I care? You're an idiot.

New Experiences

Many of the items on the list involve invoking the novelty circuits in your brain. Even if the experience is not a laugh-riot, simply exploring some new experience will give your day a boost.

It could be a day experiencing the awe or the peace to be found in nature. Realizing how small you are reminds you that your problems are also very small in the cosmic view of things.
That's how I feel at Niagara Falls or when visiting a resident of Okefenokee Swamp, GA.

For me, anything that involves mountains, swiftly-moving water or animals gets my brain crackling with the right chemicals. My first meeting and five subsequent dates with my future husband were all-day affairs, in the following order: the Oregon Zoo, Northwest Trek [a wildlife park], the Oregon Museum of Science & Industry, the Tacoma Zoo and Aquarium & the Seattle Zoo. Do you see a pattern? Psychologists say that you are more likely to fall in love with someone if your serotonin circuits are buzzing, so doing something new and exciting will make the person you're with buzz in your brain too.

You'll never know what you could fall in love with until you try it, enough times to see if your heart sings when you do it. Your first experience may be too filled with fear of failure or criticism for you to truly evaluate what your heart wants. My 2008 book Take Back Your Lost Heart is a great companion to this book, as is my Creative Chakras class.

Now that you have worked your way through the easy cures, your mild case may be easing. If you have a moderate to severe case, you will need more. Keep going to the next chapter.

Chapter 3

Cures That Require Commitment, But Not Much Money – Essential for Moderate to Severe Cases

The cures in this chapter will not cost you much money, but they will require commitment. You have to want to get well really badly to actually implement them. You have to put things in your daily calendar and weekly calendar and move heaven and earth to make them happen. If you slip, slack off or fall down, you forgive yourself and just get back to it. A Chinese proverb tells us that falling down seven times and getting up eight times will get us to the finish line. In this case, you WILL get your SAD under control.

Start with the Holy Trio:

1. Nutrition [don't try, do]
2. Sleep for at least 7 hours every night [don't try, do]
3. Exercise every day [without fail, no excuses]

Everyone knows that being 20% over your normal weight is a significant danger. By that I mean as determined by standard tables, not the unrealistic weight that you achieved as a teenager, or the inflated overweight that you've been telling yourself is OK. Overweight is related to every preventab**le form** of death, including cancer [particularly in women], slow terrible deaths from heart disease, and stokes that will leave us totally paralyzed or mentally vegetables. **Not getting enough sleep has been shown to increase cancer rates and heart disease death rates**, and I'm not talking about the 85+ set. I paint this stark picture because we have to get out of denial. People who exercise, sleep and eat as described below not only will almost certainly live longer, they will have a short illness prior to death. People who don't exercise, sleep and eat carefully are most likely to have a long, slow decline in functioning a decade sooner. **Do you want to have a long, slow, lingering death?**

`This is a serious question, so please answer it seriously

It is frequently, but not always, men who tell me that they want to eat whatever they want and choose not to exercise, and don't care if they die sooner and live sicker. They're full of horse-hockey. They live like idiots and then get quadruple bypasses and are scared witless of dying. I have never in my almost six decades of life met anyone who has spent their life making stupid choices, based on what feels good at the moment, and then approached death with gleeful anticipation of their demise. What they really mean is that they are hoping that 2+2 doesn't really add up to 4. They – does that include you? - are in denial. Americans are spending millions of dollars of taxpayer and insurance rate-payer money to eke out a few more weeks or even days of continued miserable, gasping or pain-wracked existence at the end of life. We are desperate to not die. We will do anything to hold back the day of transition. No one is seriously making the choice to die young or die in miserable pain. What we are, are emotional five-year olds, having a tantrum when the big bad adult tells us that we have to do something or can't have something.

I need to say something, with great respect for your personal decision-making powers.

Grow up.

There are no excuses. Go to the CDC website, MedLine or another reputable health website or book [you know, those things with paper in them, so 20th Century, but they are nice for when you are soaking in your friend's hot tub] and find some exercises that you will commit to for every day. The book <u>You: On a Diet</u>, by Drs. Roisen and Oz, has very nice basic exercises that nearly anyone can do. I do a mix of yoga, hand weights, treadmill and walking outdoors on different days. I join a gym in the bleak midwinter. I put the time slot in my daily calendar and if I have a crisis and have to move it, I move it, not erase it. Yoga is not only good for building muscles, it also acts as a meditation/prayer period. I love two--fers. Twice a month, I go contra or English country dancing. It's not intellectually challenging, and boy is it ever aerobic.

An interesting way to get another two-fer is to join a gym for the winter months. Find a place with a heated indoor pool and a sauna or hot tub, aqua aerobics and no joining fee. Fall is good because no one is interested in joining a gym then. They are hungry for new members. Don't sign any kind of contract unless you can cancel at any time and do not, if you value your sanity, allow them to auto-debit from your bank account. You can challenge a fraudulent credit card billing much easier . My local gym has a heated pool and I join in the bleak midwinter, which in my miserable climate lasts for most of ten months. I get my exercise, I get to pretend I'm paddling in the South Pacific and I get warm.

As for **sleep**, I know that many of us are too overwhelmed with responsibilities to even consider sleeping more. We may be so jangled on stimulants and anxiety that we think we can never achieve even seven hours. The reality is that **sleep discipline can be learn**ed. Go to the Resources appendix; you can go to your local public library and come home with an armful. Be prepared to take notes. Make one change at a time and commit to it. Why? Well, in addition to cancer and other ways of dying young, lack of sleep has also been linked to some REALLY serious stuff, like hair loss, poor skin, sagging wrinkles and sex problems.

Where to start with Exercise:

- The Roisen/Oz books have good exercise routines that nearly everyone can do.

- Walk for 20 minutes every day. Walk around your block or your workplace. Look at my ideas for getting sun; they include ways to walk around and look like you're working.

- You can walk at malls during bad weather. Get a group together with at least one other person from your church, neighborhood, etc. and you are both less likely to make excuses. Find senior friends. They are less likely to flake out than parents of young children or people who are desperately trying to make partner at their law firm.

- Buy a treadmill on Craig's List in February – June, when people are dumping the gifts that they are not using. I got a brand-new treadmill for only $100. I walk while I watch a video. [This is a good reward for a video addict, especially if it is coupled with a prohibition on video watching until the daily exercise is complete.] Treadmilling is just walking. If you can walk, this is a good choice.

• If you are disabled, there are seated exercise classes on PBS and several cable channels. You can also buy adaptive exercise DVDs; libraries can get them for you on Interlibrary Loan.

• Buy cheap light weights. Start with 5 lbs. I'm serious. Even if you are a man, if you are starting from a place of not much exercise, your muscles need to start from scratch. Find a book that shows basic moves and do them VERY SLOWLY. A light weight moved very slowly will really give your muscles a workout. Why do so many people like to do exercises quickly? Two reasons, basically: you feel like you are doing more if you are moving quickly and panting dramatically and – this is the big one – you don't have to work the muscles as hard when you move quickly. Are you surprised? An arm that is moving slowly is isolating muscles. You can't use your back and torso muscles to help you if you are moving your arm slowly. Try it – VERY SLOWLY. See how quickly the muscle tires! The best payoff? Those 5 pound weights cost very little. Buy them used. You can move to 8 lbs. when you can do five sets on each muscle without feeling the burn.

If you are a woman and are afraid you'll lose your feminine appeal with strong muscles, I know what you are talking about. Dumb men will be turned off by obvious muscles. The good news is that unless you are simultaneously taking testosterone supplements [please don't!], *your muscles will never bulge.* Men's muscles bulge because testosterone makes the muscle cells move away from each other; in other words, they just LOOK bigger. **A woman as strong as a Navy SEAL will never have arms and legs that bulge like a man's. So there goes another excuse for not exercising**.

The Bottom Line on Exercise:

Do you brush your teeth at least 5 days/week? Why?

Yes, I know that you want more control over your life. You want to be able to say NO to something that you don't want to do, because you don't think that you can say NO to your boss, your spouse, your kids or your father-in-law.

The reality is that moving your body for at least 20 minutes most days is as non-negotiable as brushing your teeth. If you really brush them, it is because you put taking care of your teeth in the Have To, No Options category. [If all you cared about was bad breath, you could swish mouthwash 3 times a day and never brush.] If you don't brush and floss, you'll lose your teeth. If you don't exercise, you'll lose your life. So put exercise in the Have To, No Options category. Every time the "I don't want to" emotion gets started, cut it off. It's not about wanting to. It's not about choice. It's a Have To, Period. When you release the need to ask yourself if you want to, you release so much emotional energy. It will become as automatic as brushing yc you keep at it. It took your parents years to get the Brush Your Teeth habit so well established in brain that you can't imagine going to work with a gummy mouth.

Meditate every day for 10 minutes in the AM and 10 minutes before you go to sleep. If you are inclined to prayer, do that for another 10 minutes before you retire.

My book Take Back Your Lost Heart: A Toolkit for Living With Courage & Caring in the Turbulent 21st Century (2008) has a chapter of meditation instruction. Appendix A has more recommended books. If you are thinking that **meditation** is too hard, test that hypothesis with hard facts. One unsuccessful experience can't be allowed to convince you that what millions of people use every day won't work for you. I teach 12 completely different types of meditation; you can't possibly hate them all, if you are being honest about it. People from inner city adolescents to prison inmates to harried parents have been helped by meditation. Find a form that you can commit to and make a commitment.

The book How God Changes Your Brain is an encouragement to some kind of transcendent practices every day. The changes that can happen in the structure of your brain are truly breathtaking. **Read contemplative, philosophical writings, with a positive, hopeful tone**. Having a **faith tradition** or a habit of thinking philosophically has a clinical history of **lifting depression** because it can change the biochemistry of your brain in some way, in all but the most severe cases. As always, stay away from the "angry God" people, places and literature. Getting together with your church/temple/philosophy group for fun, a service project or just discussing Amazing Grace is a great way to lift the dark chemistry.

Consider **yoga**. Yoga is one of the most effective two-fers on the planet. Millions of Americans have embraced yoga for muscular development, exercise and stress reduction. It is wonderful for this purpose. There is a terrific book about men and yoga that has a football player on the cover. Real Men Do Yoga shows the Y-chromosome crowd exactly how to use the muscle-building potential of yoga.

So, yes, yoga is great for exercise, which boosts serotonin and therefore mood.

But yoga is much more valuable than that. Yoga also has a spiritual component. **The spiritual value of yoga is not in any religious label.** The spiritual value of yoga, Reiki and any other practice that leads your brain into a place where the barriers between Me and the Rest of Reality dissolve away, in which I become one with the universe at a very real level, is that getting to this place of Oneness is the single most powerful action you take in your hopefully-long lifetime. Every time you meet the Universe in this place of Oneness is a time when your serotonin levels leap upward like a soaring eagle and your body and spirit focus furiously on renewal and creativity. These moments are golden, on every level that exists. Your religion or lack of it exists in the realm of concepts and words. Real Truth exists beyond words. The time that you spend in Truth, in wordless union with transcendent existence, changes your biochemistry more effectively and more permanently than any drug can. A person with a true mental illness cannot achieve this oneness. Those of us with seasonal depression can.

I recommend that you try various forms of yoga, through DVDs and live classes, and all the types of meditation in Take Back Your Lost Heart or Meditation for Wimps, until you find a practice that works for you. Realize that both yoga and meditation will feel uncomfortable and "I don't wanna" will surface. Give a particular practice a fair trial before you abandon it. Meditation sometimes taps into long-ago unhealed wounds and your unconscious will put up resistance to having the pain come out to the light of day. If you have a moderate to severe case of SAD, a good therapist, hypnotherapist or similar professional can really make a difference in helping you to clear out the emotional poisons that can be making your biochemical problem worse.

Reiki Energy Healing – Relaxation on Demand

Reiki energy healing will leave you relaxed and at peace. You can go to a practitioner for a session and you can also take classes and learn to reiki yourself. It's not like massage; no one touches your body except for your head and feet, and you stay comfortable and clothed at all times. The practitioner is opening a special channel so that life-force energy can move from the universe, through her/his body and into yours.

Sound woo-woo? It's a staple in many hospitals and cancer centers these days because while we don't know exactly how it operates, there is growing clinical evidence that it does work. It's very likely that reiki energy is positively impacting immune system function. At the very least, it induces a deep relaxation; we have known for a long time that deep relaxation promotes health and healing in a variety of illnesses and conditions.

My website www.soaringreiki.com has a collection of recent clinical studies available right on the home page. www.reiki.org also has reputable information, prepared by William Lee Rand, one of the most honored names in the profession. I am a Reiki Master and teacher. I encourage you to look into Reiki treatments and training because I have a high level of confidence in its efficacy. Some practitioners are better, and more ethical, than others. I am happy to answer any questions you may have about particular practitioners, and there are two excellent books in the Resources. If you learn Reiki you will have a tool that can de-stress you when you need it, completely under your own control.

Meditation + Exercise: Avoiding Weight Gain in Winter

ople will tell you that Christmas, Thanksgiving and New Years are the three reasons why you gain weight er. If only it were as simple as sucking up your willpower! Certainly, learning how to say "That looks us! Enjoy! I have to get this to the printer right away!" and running away as quickly as possible is a fensive skill. But that is not the major cause of weight gain. Hermits who live in caves and mutter ug!" through November and December still gain weight if they have European ancestry.

Why is European ancestry such a liability? Your metabolism slows down in winter. You are the descendent of a human being who was born with an aberration in their metabolism. They went into semi-hibernation during the cold, dark season. And because lowering your metabolism gives you a better chance to survive the cold, dark season when plants don't grow and animals are harder to hunt, that aberration survived and left healthier children who also survived. The person who could survive with less food only needed to have a small drop in daily caloric needs to make a difference. And ten thousand years later, the gene that makes one's metabolic rate dive in winter has become very common among folks whose ancestors evolved in Europe and other cold places like Siberia and Tierra del Fuego. It is the drop in light levels that signals your brain to lower your metabolic rate. [It's actually more complicated than that, involving more organs. Email me for details.] Even SAD-S sufferers need enough light in winter to prevent them from weight gain, if they have the dreaded ancestry.

Dump the emotional garbage in your Journal before you go to sleep AND
Use cognitive/behavioral techniques that are generic to anyone experiencing depression

My book Take Back Your Lost Heart: A Toolkit for Living With Courage & Caring in the Turbulent 21st Century (2008) has three whole chapters devoted to this. Here is a short excerpt:

1. Dump the Toxic Garbage

Start a **Feelings Journal** and work at it at least every other evening. Talk to a divine presence or talk to your own scared inner child or inner wisdom, perhaps as you walk, every day. Write whatever you are truly feeling. Get nasty; get real. Do NOT let your "trying to look good" social self edit this. *And for heaven's sake, do NOT, no matter how much you love someone, let them see your journal. This law is eternal and you flout it at your extreme peril.* If your subconscious mind knows that it will be evaluated, it will not be honest with you. And you need to dump your poison. This needn't take more than 15 minutes a day, but you must focus on it, without interruptions, to get the full benefit for mind and body.

Do **structured sentence completions**: [My clients say this one alone can turn your life around, by getting the emotions out of your body and on to the page.] Dump the Garbage every day for a month and see what happens!

I am angry [I resent]

I am sad

I am ashamed

I am happy

I want

I intend

2. Talk to your inner child (who is feeling scared and unloved) whenever a work situation or an interpersonal ruckus raises your stress level. It really makes a difference. Feel the part of you that is angry – it's probably scared. Advanced Reiki techniques and hypnotherapy are two of the most effective ways to get control of your life by calming your frightened inner child.

Here is an exercise that I like to do with my clients. I've adapted this from the work of the estimable Martha Beck [run out and buy all her books right now], who is a life coach like me. You are going to separate your thinking, logical mind from your feeling, intuitive mind. Or your mind from your body. Or your conscious mind from your subconscious mind. Or your wise adult and your child.

On the left side of the page, have your adult ask these two questions: *What do you need?* Your child will blast you with resentment, frustration and dissatisfaction. Write it all down on the right side of the paper. Don't defend or get angry back. Just keep writing. When the right side is ready to wind down, ask your next question: *What can I do to make you happy?* Your child will take a while, but eventually there will be something. Just keep writing on the right side, and on the left side, asking only clarifying questions or make suggestions for things you can do to make your body/child/subconscious happy. In my case, having some time off to do creative things or going out to the craft store or the thrift store for a little low-level retail fun, or watching a movie, or getting some help with an onerous chore, will crop up as solutions. If your child wants an around the world cruise, ask how the cruise will make her happy. Drill down until you know: does she just need a vacation [you could do a cheaper one]; need some sun [amen, sister, amen]; want to laugh and do sports; want some couple time. That's what the cruise will really give you. See if you can give it yourself some other, do-able way.

3. Describe the Challenge. This is a left-brain technique, for those of you who are more comfortable thinking than feeling. Write down exactly what you are trying to decide. Now write down all the pros and cons and all the things you know about what you are trying to accomplish, *without insisting on an instant answer,* to give your inner wisdom something to "chew on."

Answers are most likely to come while your conscious, logical mind is quiet, for example, while you are meditating or exercising. You are not forcing answers to come on your timetable; you are asking for guidance in the Universe's own good time. I strongly encourage you to work through my book, or pick one of the excellent books on forgiveness in Resources.

Service projects

We've discussed service projects before. If you have serious SAD, service can really help, by taking you out of the tendency to make your misery more acute by noticing it.

Be very clear about what I am saying! You are NOT creating your biochemical problem. You can NOT make your biochemical problem go away by mind control. What you can do is prevent it from getting worse than it needs to be.

Service can get you involved with the world, which itself boosts serotonin. You just have to flog yourself out the door. Put up signs and sticky-notes. Choose what you care about most, and get involved:

- Animals. Do you want to cuddle them, give them Reiki, take them for walks or train them? Can you commit to poop-clearing as well? Do you prefer to help wild animals? Animal shelters or wild-animal parks, rescue organizations of every ilk need help.

- Adults, families, children, seniors. Are there demographics of people you feel especially drawn to? Do you want to interact with them directly, as in a soup kitchen, or would you prefer to create web sites, update files or hold people's hands and listen to them reminisce? Would you like to teach children reading or math? Your city and county have volunteer hotlines. Call.

- Public cleanups or special events. These can be a great way to get out if you prefer one-shot events. There are walks to raise money for this and bake-offs to raise money for that. The environmental cleanups give you some great exercise as well.

- CERT, NET, ham groups and emergency preparedness. There's nothing better than preparing to be a hero and practicing to be a hero, except actually being a hero when the emergency strikes. You already are a community hero every time you pay your property and other taxes joyfully and with a good heart; you are the community hero who feeds the hungry kids and keeps the seniors from freezing to death and everyone from dying of preventable diseases. This is just another shot of SuperHero juice.

In the next chapter, we will transition to the cures that will cost [illegible] case of SAD-W, these are the cures that will pack the biggest ba[illegible] someone turned on the light in your life.

Chapter 4

Cures That Require Both Time & Money – Essential for Severe Cases & Very Helpful for Moderate Cases

This collection of ideas requires more time or money – although not an excessive amount of either – and will give you the strongest, fastest journey out of SAD. They all involve giving your body what it desperately craves – some serious light.

Let's start with the easiest, least expensive option:

Buy a Light Box with enough lumens to really do the job, and use it every day, religiously, for as long as you need to, to get results**.** In early Fall, ten minutes will do me. In the bleak midwinter, I need an hour or more.

Since models and brands change quickly, I won't make specific recommendations. I WILL suggest that you read reviews with a careful and critical eye. I found a collection of products online at Amazon, read the user reviews, then researched them in various online medical publications.

- You need a professional lightbox that puts out **10,000 lumens**.
- Some research indicates that it is the blue part of the spectrum that is most effective, hence the Blue Light craze.

I bought an **Apollo Go-Lite** because it has good reviews as to actual output, as tested by an independent laboratory, and user reviews tell me it is reliable. It is also small and portable so I can take it with me. Spread your fingers out; the size of your hand is the size of my lightbox. I have used this model for two years.

When attending seminars and classes during the winter, I can plug it in and prop it by my desk or table and get my required therapy during breaks and – depending how tightly-packed the attendees are – even during the lecture or demos. It cost around $200 and should last for four years, the way I use it. The box's lifetime will be longer or shorter depending on how much therapy you need every day.

Pick a lightbox that is easy to use because if it isn't you'll have excuses for not using it. A cheaper product that never gets used is a total waste of money. Remember – money is a concept on two axes: there is what you paid for it and there is the value that the product gives you. Be realistic about the latter. My product cost me $200 and has given me two years of income-generation. I am a consultant so my income is directly related to how much I work. Get depressed and my income goes down. But there is more to it. If I get depressed, I am going to gain weight. What is that going to cost me? I am going to rely on retail therapy to cheer me up. What will that cost? I will be buying pharmaceuticals or getting therapy. What will that cost? Or I will be torpedoing my marriage. [Listen to me, guys. Women DO signal their pissossity for years before they finally take off and leave you with half your financial resources, or less if you have children to support.] What will losing your marriage cost you, in direct costs and the long-term emotional costs? What is the total that you have so far?

What is $200 as a percentage of the amount of income you will save, or the expenses you will not incur? Put the total over 200 and you get a Return on Investment [ROI] for the cost of the lightbox. What number did you get? If you're both honest and like most of us, it's pretty dang big.

How to use a lightbox: Read the instructions carefully!!

My Go-Lite has simple Power and then Light buttons, and I can program specific lengths of time.

DON'T stare directly into the light. You set it off to the side, so you can see it in the corner of your eye. The light needs to get through your pupils and the indirect location works perfectly. Don't have it out of your line of sight or you won't get any benefit. I put it on my desk when I am working in the office.

Most of my clients work in offices and find it easy to set up a small lightbox in their cubicles.

People who spend most of the day in their car need to use it during lunch break or before they start the day. Combine it with another activity – perhaps your early AM meditation.

If you glance directly at it by accident, you will probably experience a short stint of seeing the LEDs before your eyes in the opposite colors of the spectrum. This effect fades away. I researched my lightbox and am convinced that this model is not harmful. Therapeutic lightboxes in general are designed to not harm you if you follow the instructions. I would keep it away from young children or persons of any age who are in oppositional-defiant mode [refuse to listen to any restrictions or instructions]. If you want to hurt yourself, you can probably find a way to do so with any product.

Other ways to get light include lightboxes that you essentially wear as a hat. The light streams down from above your eyes. The reviews that I have seen aren't as positive about these as they are about the standard lightboxes, but the technology is constantly advancing, so – collect accurate data and make a decision on that basis.

How long? Essentially, as long as you need, and individuals differ. Most people need an hour or more when the dark days follow each other for weeks. If you get a sunny or semi-sunny day, you will probably need less on the day after. What I recommend is that you start with small doses and keep increasing it until you get relief. Nearly everyone gets relief from light therapy sooner or later.

The key is not to stint! Start with 10-15 minutes of light therapy in the fall. If you wait until your depression is noticeable, you have gotten yourself into a deep hole and you will need more therapy to get out of it than you would have needed if you didn't get your self into such poor shape. So stop looking for ways to convince yourself that you're not really sick, suck it up and do the therapy. If you are starting in the deep winter, or if you are starting from a place where you are already affected, start with 30 minutes and jump to 60 minutes within a week.

Do light therapy every day!

What about the weekend? Your body needs light on the weekend, too. Set up your lightbox on the breakfast table, or anywhere else you can squeeze out some space.

What time of day? Remember that the light is revving up your body and you won't have any trouble realizing that morning is best, as soon after you get up as possible. Meditate with your eyes open and you get a two-fer: light therapy and starting your day with the calm, powerful emotional state that has nothing but good effects all day. If you use your lightbox in the late afternoon, you may have trouble falling asleep before midnight, or later.

If you are one of the minority that wakes up with no symptoms of SAD-W but crashes later in the day, then light therapy in the afternoon may be the ticket. If you find that you fit this category and you don't have insomnia problems, then put the light therapy in your daily appointments for right after lunch or the last hour of your workday. Plan the light therapy for the hours BEFORE you find yourself crashing.

Does it have to be continuous time? No, apparently not. Your pineal gland and other systems need the light, but it can come in segments. Here's why I caution against this practice, and encourage you to turn it on for your full time first thing in the AM: you're more likely to actually do the time if you carve out the timeslot and don't invade it. People who postpone light therapy to take care of other needs are like people who postpone a planned exercise period. They hardly ever really come back to it. Some other crisis erupts, and then another distraction, and then the day is over.

If there is a sudden meeting and you don't want to bring your lightbox to it – I dig the desire to not appear "sick" in these ultra-competitive times – make sure that you put your light therapy interval in your calendar for as soon as the meeting is over. If you are getting light in chunks, make sure that every one of them is in your calendar, and that you never cancel, just move, them. Remind yourself that health gives you your only reliable road to career success. You can't blow up your foundation and expect the house to stand.

Light therapy using technology is your tool for making sure that you get what you need regardless of the weather. There are some other – and fun! – ways to get light therapy that require serious time and possibly some money too.

Take day trips to a sunny place on your days off, as often as possible. If it keeps raining on the weekends, take a vacation or sick day. Visit your doctor 1st thing in the morning to satisfy the idiots at your company's HR department and then drive, drive, drive until the sun comes out. This is me on the boardwalk in Redondo, Washington, on an uncommonly sunny day in January.

Where I live in Western Washington, I can find sun if I cross the Cascade Mountains. Once I climb over the Snoqualmie Pass to the central plateau beyond, a magical transformation occurs. The sun comes out, the eternal rain stops, my mood brightens. My client Bill is a remodeling contractor and has a hard time getting lightbox time. He takes a weekend in Yakima every month, to keep himself out of SAD. To do that, you have to drive south for two hours, then east for an hour. He could make that a daytrip, but he stays with friends so his weekends cost him only gas money. His wife and kids love the husband and father who comes back.

It's very easy to tell yourself, as you can with all the cures in this chapter, that **you don't have the time or the money**. You probably don't, as long as you label these daytrips as Vacation or Extras or Optional. What happens if you label it, to yourself and everyone else, over and over and over again, as Critical Medical Expense? Does your family resent the co-pay on your mammogram or colonoscopy? Is your spouse finding the money to buy big-screen TVs, electronic gadgets, shoes, new clothes, power tools or every new toy the kids ask for? *What does that say about who and what is most important in their life?*

Don't be a martyr. You'll end up costing everyone twice the money if you don't treat your seasonal depression effectively. And that lazy grab for antidepressants that I can hear you considering? Does your spouse want a zonked-out sexually-dysfunctional zombie? Really, really think about your priorities and your life before you make this decision.

Take your annual vacation in mid-winter to a sunny location, for as long as you can afford.

This is Merchant's Millpond State Park, NC.

Northern New Mexico, southern Texas, Florida, Georgia, southern California and many tropical islands have sunny skies during the Northern Hemisphere's winter.

This isn't as trivial an issue as you might think at first. You are going to have to adjust people's expectations, as I explained in earlier chapters. You need to be taking vacations that get you OUT of Dodge during the dark months, not in the summer when life is tolerable where you are paying a mortgage for lodging. Work with a counselor, a life coach or related mental health professional to help you to create a life in which your needs matter to the people around you, and your needs get attended to.

It has been scientifically proven that a family in which the parents are in charge – and I mean really, emotionally in charge, not responding to manipulation – is vastly healthier and happier for everyone, including the children ultimately, compared to a family in which the children's desires are the driving force.

An adult-centered marriage is stronger and an adult-driven family is both stronger and creates stronger children than a family where the kids, with their limited wisdom, are driving the bus. Similarly, adults who have a strong sense of self, and can take care of their health needs with a loving caress for the other adults and children in their lives, raise children who are equally warm, loving and willing o take responsibility for their choices and their needs, and who have empathy and commitment to helping others get their needs met.

Short version: Do your best to get the family with you on this plan. If you can't, go yourself.

In the next chapter, we'll explore the "cures" that are at best useless and at worst can kill you.

Chapter 5

"Cures" That Might Tempt You Because They Are Cheap or Easy – But Don't Work or Could be Dangerous

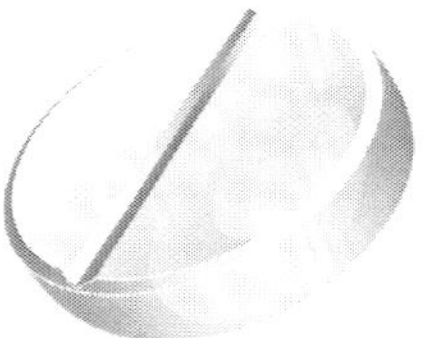

This is my least favorite chapter, for a variety of reasons. Firstly, I hate to rain on anyone's parade, so spending time chronicling what doesn't work is not my idea of fun. Ignorance is bliss, y'all, and I would be happy to leave folks in bliss, except for one factor: ignorance can get you killed. Which brings me to Secondly: I have had clients and potential clients who have gone down this road, and the story always ends badly.

Ask anyone. I refuse to go to movies unless I am sure that everyone's going to end up happy at the end. I spend 99% of my time in reality, and I don't need any more sadness. So I don't enjoy dwelling on what doesn't work. On the other hand, if I don't discuss this subject, I am being irresponsible. So here goes.

Let's start with some things that don't work but will do nothing worse than waste your money and leave you still miserable.

Ordinary light bulbs advertised as "full spectrum" may have a health benefit for people without SAD, although there are no reputable studies that say so. What's for sure is that the wattage of these bulbs is way too low to do anything for you. The only kind of light that will make any difference is the 10,000 lumens therapeutic lights from solid, reputable companies that are listed in Chapter 4.

Untested, exotic herbs. The herbs that have a track record for treating or ameliorating depression are a good bet. Don't take anything that hasn't been studied thoroughly in studies conducted by someone other than the manufacturer. Something can make you **feel better and be wrecking your [only, crucial] liver, like kava kava did.**

The next category of Please Don't Do This is the kind of "cure" that has a high probability of killing you.

The poster child for this choice is the oh-so-seductive **tanning salon.** The longer you have gone without sun, and the more miserable you feel, the more seductive this option is.

After all, it DOES make you feel good. When 20-something tanners in Florida are interviewed, the "looking good" response is very popular. Talk to tanners in January in any of the northern cloud-socked states, and you hear a different story: it makes them **feel** better. Light DOES relieve depression, and most of the tan-seekers are suffering from mild to moderate cases of SAD, in my opinion.

It makes sense that tanning would have a beneficial effect on mood. The light soaks into your skin, your body responds with a surge of Vitamin D production. The light gets through your closed eyelids and the pineal responds with serotonin. What's not to love?

What's not to love?

In a word, **melanoma**. The most common form of skin cancer, basal cell carcinoma, is quite common in light-skinned people and is easily curable for people with access to affordable health care. Most basal cell cancers grow so slowly that before the cells make contact with the blood system – that lovely highway to metastasis – the person has noticed the funny spot that's growing and gets the cancer removed. Rates are increasing as people live longer [more cumulative sun exposure in a longer lifespan] and as people do stupid things like sun-bathe and go to tanning salons. Only a serious hypochondriac, or someone with no health care access at all, would be frightened about basal cell carcinoma. In fact, it grows so slowly that if you have no health care and you see a suspicious mole, you have time to look around you and find someone with health insurance to marry, or borrow some money from a friend or relative, or find a low-cost state or private insurance plan and wait six months for the coverage to kick in.

Not so with melanoma. This is a nasty customer on two fronts:

- It metastases rapidly and – just to make life really fun –
- It is notoriously resistant to chemotherapy.

Another category of "cures" that I want to discourage is the **lazy grab for anti-depressants by SAD sufferers – and their doctors.**

Now, make sure that you hear this clearly: ***I am very, very grateful for the existence of effective pharmaceutical aid for serious psychiatric illnesses. People who would have been doomed to eternal institutionalization have had their lives restored to them. Some products are genuine miracles and blessings. For people who genuinely need anti-depressants, they can be life-savers.***

The problem with anti-depressants is not the folks with serious psychiatric illnesses who are taking them. The problem with anti-depressants is the literally millions of people who are taking them who DON'T need to be taking them. Side-effects range from moderate to severe. If there is a crucial need for them, the side-effects are the price you pay for salvation. If you are taking heavy-duty medicine because either you are too lazy to do the things that you need to do to eliminate the depression without drugs, or you have a doctor who is too timid or lazy to stand up to you when you are demanding a quick-fix pill, then that is a problem

Mild to moderate depression, which is what most SAD qualify as, can be cured with **30 minutes with a light box, 30 minutes of daily exercise, a careful diet of whole grains & vegetables, and daily meditation or prayer.** If you have a medical practitioner that you are comfortable with, talk over your medication use. Start engaging in the non-drug regimen alongside your medication, to demonstrate that you will stay with the exercise, diet and meditation or prayer. After you have done that for six months with no more than an occasional slide, see if trying to fly without the drugs makes sense.

If you don't have a medical professional that you can have a frank conversation with, or who is not willing to let you try any kind of dedicated and serious non-drug experiment, you might want to consider finding a medical practitioner who will act as your partner in wellness. ***If you are taking medication, please do NOT***

stop taking the medication abruptly. Many anti-depressants have dangerous effects if you stop them abruptly.

Remember: **ideology has no place in managing your health**! A particular doctor's pro-meds ideology and your best friends never-take-meds ideology are equally dangerous and foolish. My own philosophy is to learn as much as possible from reputable sources, then try experiments with low chances of harming me. I love some individual MDs, NDs, ANPs and Reiki, acupuncture and massage practitioners. I don't make blanket judgments about one type of health care being better than another. I love some medications, including the ones I take, have cheerfully embraced some surgeries, and all forms of meditation and yoga. I urge everyone to maintain an open mind and let ideologies starve to death from lack of feeding.

One ideology that can harm you, and might even kill you, is ignoring biochemistry entirely. Stay away from:

- Toughing it out [this is not masculinity; it's stupidity]
- Using positive thinking, mind control, The Secret or any similar philosophy as an exclusive cure, especially if there is an implied criticism of YOU if the cure doesn't work.

Reading the next chapter will give you tools to help with SAD-S. SAD-W sufferers might get some interesting ideas as well, either in terms of cures or in terms of what to avoid. Both are useful.

Chapter 6

Dealing with Summer SAD

Fewer people suffer from the summer form of SAD, but their suffering is no less severe. Summer sufferers are exhilarated by cooler weather. While no one could possibly enjoy six months of continual nor'easters, summer SAD sufferers do chirp along happily and productively in a Pacific Northwest-style climate, which is grey and drizzly for at least half of the year.

Before we get to therapies, let's remember that summer SAD sufferers, no matter how much they may prefer the cool and drizzle, do have to keep some of the winter SAD therapies in mind. Why ever would that be, you ask? Well, think about it. No matter what season of SAD you have, or even if you are unaffected by SAD at all, you are a human being. All of us have some things in common.

- We need strong bones.

You need to ingest adequate calcium and magnesium, as well as Vitamin D3. You need to get 15 minutes of light onto your bare skin every day, if possible. I know that light tends to increase your depression, but 15 minutes per day will not bring you down. It will allow your skin to manufacture D3 precursors from cholesterol D, and that is very, very good news indeed. All of us need lots of Vitamin D, and if you love cool, overcast days, there is a real danger that you won't remember to take care of your bones. Supplements are not as effective as real sun for this.

➢ Our eyes need light.

You need to have that 15 minutes of light every day, to allow your hormone-producing organs to stay happy. If you want the details, I would love to see you in one of my Human Biology for Everyone classes, either live in the Puget Sound area, in North Carolina, in cyberspace or through CDs and tutoring. Light needs to enter your eyes, where its presence will be transmitted to your pineal gland, a pea-sized endocrine organ surrounded by brain. The pineal controls your secretion of serotonin and melatonin, the hormones that are secreted during day and night, respectively. If you don't get any light, your serotonin levels may not be as high as they need to be. Serotonin is one of the feel-good hormones. People with SAD-S need to make sure that they don't overdose on light, but you need to have some. Serotonin is also needed by several important metabolic pathways and it is an essential neurotransmitter.

So go outside and play, for your 15 minutes every day, when the sun is out.

➢ We need to exercise every day. Details are discussed in the Winter chapters.

Some other aspects of the winter regimen that you may find useful are:

Fun.

Social connections.

Eperience new places and new activities.

Ue colors, sounds and other aspects of creativity.

Just like the people who are suffering from Winter SAD!

Some specific cures for SAD-S sufferers include:

Find ways to be outdoors in spring and mid- to late fall. This is perfect time for planting and harvesting. Consider gardening and vegetable farming as engrossing and healthy activities. This is also a wonderful season for birding and photography.

➢ Plan your outdoor time in the early morning, when the light levels are indirect. This is the best time for anyone to engage in meditation walks, photography and gardening, so it's easier to get some of the sun-lovers to come with you.

➢ Create a "safe zone" for yourself in your home or apartment. *Keep the blinds at least half-closed on sunny days. Keep it cool, with a window air-conditioner. Lower the humidity with a de-humidifier. With a lower humidity, you'll feel cooler than the actual temperature. For some people with SAD-S, feeling cooler has the same beneficial effect that feeling warmer has on SAD-W sufferers.*

- *Stay in your safe zone during the middle of the day in the summer, except for the 15-20 minutes/day that you need to develop good Vitamin D for your bones.*

➢ Try out a house with north-facing windows, which gets less of the late-afternoon light and heat. No one wants to buy them so you may save a few dollars. Avoid houses with lots of south and west-facing windows. Don't be shy about pulling the shades and blinds. Let the light-lovers do so at their homes.

➢ Think about living somewhere with a compatible micro-climate. You might need a longer commute to get to your current job, but it might be easier to deal with a carpool or transit than to deal with SAD-S for six months out of every twelve. You might find a friend or co-worker to stay overnight with a day or two out of the week, while you come home the rest of the days.

Think about living in a coastal area, where fog is common. This cuts the amount of daylight that summer days will inflict on you. Look at New England to Labrador and from Northwest California to Vancouver Island. The Great Lakes area has foggy mornings in summer as do many river valleys.

Think about mountain towns and places in the foothills. Ask and ask and ask some more. Chamber of Commerce. Realtors. Someone will know of a microclimate that is cool and shady.

North Dakota has a perennially low unemployment rate. The weather stinks, by a sun-lover's standards, so competition for highly-skilled jobs is lessened.

➢ Think about jobs where you can travel or telecommute, thereby allowing you to choose a nicely damp and foggy home. You would be surprised at how many campgrounds have WiFi and power outlets these days, not to mention every Mom-and-Pop budget motel. *Spend the money for a good career or life coach. I am one. There are others. Don't convince yourself that you can't afford it until you have asked a lot of questions.*

➢ Kids can guilt-trip you into doing what they love, even if it makes you sick. Don't fall into this trap! Let someone else take the kids on a summer vacation, unless they inherited your DNA and need less light as well. *Get someone to take the kids to play on the beach or milk the cows while you have some alone time indoors.*

➢ Avoid summer barbeques. If you think you absolutely have to attend or host one, lie down until that belief fades. I haven't attended one in decades and I still have friends and family who love me. If you go, there are lots of jobs that require staying in the kitchen or indoors and the sun-lovers hate them so you won't have any competition. For heaven's sake, don't host one alone!

Be careful with summertime family reunions. The parents who let their kids dictate their decisions are a problem, as are the parents who are determined to relive their childhood memories. Try to sell folks on the lower costs of off-season vacations, particularly fall. Fall color, too! Tell people that the sun gives you a headache and stay indoors and make beds.

➢ Make summer your time to visit museums – a typical indoor activity that the sun-lowers relegate to late fall and winter.

➢ Take your family vacation to someplace where the weather is going to be cool and cloudy. New Zealand in July comes to mind. When you travel in the season when most people stay away, you can save a bundle on airfare and accommodations. Spring and fall are also great times to avoid high light levels, and save a bundle.

Know what frames and analogies to use: Ordinarily caring people can be disrespectful if they don't understand your problem. **Most people are not stupid enough to tell a diabetic that they could wish away their metabolic problem**, so you might say your problem is metabolic like diabetes. It requires special diet, special meditations, daily exercise and all the rest of your health-management program.

If you are dealing with insensitive know-it-alls, DON'T tell them that you have seasonal depression. Don't argue with people who will state authoritatively – on the basis of their brother's, their co-worker's, their mother's, their child's or even their own experience – what you should, could or must do, to make your illness instantly disappear. State, in a firm, commanding tone, that you have received expert medical advice and change the subject. If they persist, look them right in the eye and tell them that your health is a private matter and none of their business. Keep repeating it as they bluster, until they finally retreat.

If you encounter anyone who tries to tell you that you're not entitled to take care of your physical health as a physical health problem, you need to keep reminding yourself that physiology is not susceptible to Positive Thinking cures alone. If you are a SAD-S sufferer, you will receive repeated admonitions to "get out in the sunshine; you're feel better!" You can get barraged with so many "change your mind" messages that you start to doubt your own senses and sanity. Dealing with loved ones who are falling down in the caring about one's welfare department is particularly hard to bear. Hold on to the one uncontestable fact: **You are not insane. You are a person with a physiological problem who is doing her darndest to stay well.** And get back to your cures.

Now it is time to create a customized plan that will work for YOU!

Chapter 7

Making a Powerful Plan to Beat Your Seasonal Blues

We are all unique. What will serve my needs, might not serve yours. Your goal will undoubtedly be to start with the ideas that are suggested for mild cases and work your way up the ladder of cost and commitment until you reach the combination of options that alleviates your symptoms. Some of my clients use colored pencils on this chart, outlining the solutions they have already incorporated into their lives, and the ones they are currently working on.

Winter Blues Plan

Since most SAD sufferers have SAD-W, most of this book is about you, Expand this chart so that it includes text that I may have left out, or ideas that you have generated and want to test, or have already tested and know work for you.

And remember – the greatest plan in the world is useless if you don't take action. Any action on this page, if you do it consistently, is better than a scatter-shot and haphazard effort. With the latter, you can't test what works for you and what doesn't.

For each item that you decide to work on, work at it consistently for at least 2 weeks. **DECIDE is the key word. Anything that will bring you results needs commitment. Make a decision and commit to it**

Option	**$**	**Time**	**commitment**
Nutrition/vitamin/mineral			x
Heat	DaySpa, warm house, gym	Bath	
Natural light			
-- *whenever it shines*			X
-- *travel day trips*		X	
-- *vacation 1+ wks*	X	X	
Meditate daily			X
Pray daily/read spiritual			X
Light box [10K lumens]	X $150-250	X	X
Cognitive skills	See also TBYLH		X
Social connections & fun	Low	X	x
Seek new experiences		X	X
Exercise	Low	X	x

TBYLH = Take Back Your Lost Heart.

COLOR CODE the chart above:

Color it RED if you will implement it NOW

Color it YELLOW if you will consider it.

Color it BLUE if you won't consider it at the present time.

Go to the appropriate chapter to find the cures that are associated with your choices.

You should also copy your work on the chart in Chapter 2 and have it in front of you as you make your plan.

Here is a quick way to be specific about the fun, creative, new and social items, if you just want to focus on your RED items:

My Strategies for Boosting Serotonin through Behavior

FUN	**Creative**	**Do/Learn New**	**Social**

Summer Blues Plan

As you make your summer plan, start with the easy changes first, and understand that the most effective strategies for you may not be the first two strategies you try! Go through the list and **color code your strategies**. Will you commit to this now? Will you consider it for your 2nd round? Does it not feel right at all now?

Color Red for DO it NOW

Yellow for WILL CONSIDER

BLUE for Not Now

Strategies List	COLOR
Basic nutrition for bones Ca, Mg, Vit D + 15 min of light/day	RED
Investigate how to get outdoors or take a vacation in spring/fall.	
Investigate telecommuting your job.	
Investigate moonlighting at an online job.	
Talk to a career or life coach.	
De-humidify house, get cool. Price air-conditioning.	
Create one special room of your house that fits your health needs.	
Brainstorm summer trips for kids to sunny place without you. Grandparents?	
Plan vacation to cool rainy place in summer, to avoid light.	
Investigate relocation to foggy, cloudy or rainy climate.	
Plan walks and be outdoors in early AM	
Start class in photography, birding, gardening, focusing on low-light times	
Plan museum trips for sunny weather	
Meditate every day.	
Cognitive skills, in this book, TBYLH or Resources	
Exercise – Pilates, Yoga, walking	
Pray, read spiritual/philosophical works; do Reiki.	

Other ideas – brainstorm here:

The answer, for both SAD types, could be very simple: relocate. Leave the physical environment that is making you sick.

There are some reasons why this might not be feasible for you, at least not this year.

- **you may have a very specialized career that you can only pursue in a limited number of places.** My husband, for example, does extremely specialized and amazing things with exterior paints and decals for airplanes. Either he keeps working in the Seattle area [horrible for my SAD-W] or he moves to France and works for Airbus [merde!] or we live apart [an option, at least part-time]. Unless you are equally painted into a corner [sorry, couldn't resist, dear], there probably are other options.

- **family ties**. One of my SAD clients has a mother in declining health, whom she chooses to care for. Mothers who are deeply loved can't be abandoned, but if they love us as much as we love them, they will move with us for our health, won't they? My client's mother needs a specialist, so she needs to be in a city with excellent doctors.

- **a deep love of some aspect of where we currently live**. Of course, finding a way to be healthy and happy somewhere else, and traveling to enjoy Mt. Rainier in the nice weather is an option. Perhaps your deeply-loved aspect could be loved in smaller quantities; maybe it can't. If it is a certain community, or something else that is absolutely unique, that is a dilemma. Of course, many times we think something is unique because of lack of information. I used to think many things in Northern California were unique. Then I traveled the country and found other places with similar communities, similar "vibes" and all-around livability.

- **your real estate is underwater or you haven't lived at your present location long enough to be able to sell at a profit**. Of course, you could always rent out your home and rent something in a more livable climate. A client of mine did that. After years of struggling with SAD-W, and not listening to any of my suggestions, she up and bought a new home in sunny southern California. She rented out her nice house in rainy, dark, miserable Seattle when her Californian mother had a health setback. I think that Spirit did not want her to stay in Seattle, hence her resistance to solutions that would have made a miserable situation somewhat less miserable. Her soul wanted to be gone from here, and it is.

What's the purpose of my suggesting Equally Valid Views on these subjects? I am doing what any good life coach or counselor will do for you – make sure that you are not hiding behind "I can't." Sometimes you really, truly can't. This Boeing engineer really, truly can't paint cool stuff on airplanes in Albuquerque or Maui. Most of the time, you really, truly can. Even my Boeing engineer can, if he is willing to design paints for something less fun than airplanes; chemical engineering is very flexible. In Take Back Your Lost Heart, I outline how to ask the right questions to open your mind to the range of possibilities in career, family and other aspects of life.

Here's the process for considering a new location, a new job or both:

1. brainstorm every possible and impossible idea – no censoring or "oh, that could never work."
2. investigate the most likely ones. Research online, with librarians, with real people, visit. A coach can help you think of options. This can be done in small chunks over a period of time, as long as you keep at it.
3. try out some options on the side, part-time or while on an exploratory trip.

Then make a decision, and enjoy the rest of your life!

In the Appendices, you will find Resources to consider, as well as information about the author. I've enjoyed taking this voyage of discovery with you! I look forward to meeting you in person, in cyberspace or through an audio class.

Appendix A:

Resources

By no means the Last Word on either depression or SAD, these are some resources that I use with my own clients.

Albert, Katherine A., MD. (1996) Get a Good Night's Sleep: An Expert on Sleep Disorders Shares the Latest Research to Help You Conquer Your Insomnia. Simon & Schuster: New York, NY.

Austin, Miriam [2003] Meditation for Wimps. Sterling Publishing: NYC
[I 100% adore this book. You must go to Amazon and order it right now.]

Beattie, Melody. (1991) A Reason to Live. Tyndale House Publishers, Inc.: Wheaton, IL.
[For anyone dealing with serious depression]

Beck, Martha. (2001) Finding Your Own North Star: Claiming the Life You Were Meant to Live. Three Rivers Press: New York, NY.

- (2003) The Joy Diet: 10 Daily Practices for a Happier Life. Crown Publishers: New York, NY.
[The Joy Diet is helpful for depression. Finding Your Own North Star can help you to uncover the emotional blocks that can be compounding a biochemical problem – or show you that you have no biochemical problem at all.]

Begley, Sharon. (2007) Train Your Mind, Change Your Brain: How a New Science Reveals Our Extraordinary Potential to Transform Ourselves. Ballantine Books: New York, NY.
[This review of new neurobiology is a must-read for anyone.]

Bloomfield, Harold H., MD, and Cooper, Robert K, PhD. (1997) How to be Safe in an Unsafe World. Crown Publishers, Inc.: New York, NY.
[Depression can exacerbate a tendency to be fearful. This is an excellent guide to doing what you can about what you can.]

Carlin, John. (2008) Invictus: Nelson Mandela and the Game That Made a Nation. Penguin Books: New York, NY. [The movie leaves out a lot. One chapter of this is enough to lift your spirits for a day. Read it through at least once, and understand why charm will always be mightier than the sword.]

Cushnir, Raphael. (2008) The One Thing Holding You Back: Unleashing the Power of Emotional Connection. Harper Collins Publishers: New York, NY.
[I don't actually like this book, but I want to be fair and ask you to read it before you dislike it too. Or else love it and find great value. I'm OK either way. ;-)]

Dalai Lama. His Holiness the XIV (2009) The Dalai lama's Little Book of Inner Peace: the Essential Life and Teachings. Hampton Roads Publishing Co, Inc.: Charlottesville, VA.
[Non-sectarian good advice on achieving inner peace.]

De Angeles, Barbara. (2005) How Did I Get Here?: Finding Your Way to Renewed Hope and Happiness When Life and Love Take Unexpected Turns. St. Martin's Griffin: New York, NY.
[The title says it all. Another good guide to unraveling the emotional issues that will definitely exacerbate a medical problem.]

Devi, Nischala Joy. (2007) The Secret power of Yoga: A Woman's Guide to the Heart and Spirit of the Yoga Sutras. Three Rivers Press: New York, NY.
[This is about the spiritual side of yoga, not a guide to poses.]

Easwaran, Eknath. (2005) Strength in the Storm: Creating Calm in Difficult Times. Nilgiri Press: Tomales, CA.
[Meditations and readings]

Elgin, Suzette Haden, Ph D. (1997) How to Disagree Without Being Disagreeable: Getting Your Point Across With the Gentle Art of Verbal Self-Defense. MJF Books: New York, NY. [If part of your depression is the people you have to deal with, this author's series of books will definitely help.]

Engel, Beverly. (2001) The Power of Apology: Healing Steps to Transform All Your Relationships. John Wiley and Sons: New York, NY.
[So many of us have depression exacerbated by unhealed wounds from the past –received or inflicted.]

Epstein, Mark, MD. Going to Pieces without Falling Apart: A Buddhist Perspective on Wholeness. Broadway Books: New York, NY. [A psychiatrist and Buddhist has a deeply-moving perspective. Probably too deep for someone with serious depression, but excellent if your brain is basically working.]

Flanagan, Beverly, MSSW. (1992) Forgiving the Unforgivable: Overcoming the Bitter legacy of Intimate Wounds. Macmillan: New York, NY.

_ (1996) Forgiving Yourself: A Step-by Step Guide to Making Peace With Your Mistakes and Getting On With Your Life. Macmillan: New York, NY.
[The 1992 book in particular needs slow careful, workbook handling. If you really do these exercises, you will transform your life.]

Katie, Byron. (2005) I Need Your Love—Is That True?: How to Stop Seeking Love, Approval and Appreciation and Start Finding Them Instead. Three Rivers Press: New York, NY.
[Byron Katie has a series of books that will radically change your thinking. This one is about depression in approval and appreciation-addicts, like most of us.]

Leo, Victoria C. [2008] Take Back Your Lost Heart. Lulu Press: Morrisville, NC
[My comprehensive overview of how to cope when life doesn't turn out like you wish: meditation, changing how you think, taking action.]

Miles, Pamela. [2006] Reiki. Tarcher/Penguin: NYC
[Miles is a leading light in making Reiki a staple of integrated medicine. Her book is a wonderful companion to Paul's. She explains how and why you should study Reiki. And she's a great human being, too.]

Muller, Wayne. (1992) Legacy of the Heart: The Spiritual Advantages of a Painful Childhood. Simon & Schuster: New York, NY. [A powerful perspective to change the exclusively poor-me, victim view, while being compassionate about the burdens of having been abused as a child.]

Myss, Caroline. (2007) Entering the Castle: Finding the Inner Path to God and Your Soul's Purpose. Free Press, a Division of Simon & Schuster, Inc.: New York, NY.
[Definitely not for the depressed, or the faint of heart, this is a journey of deep spirituality.]

__ (2007) Your Power to Create: from Wishful Thinking to True Manifestation. Sounds True: Boulder, CO.
[Forget "The Secret" and similar hogwash. This is the real creation.]

O'Connor, Richard, Ph D. (1997) Undoing Depression: What Therapy Doesn't Teach You and Medication Can't Give You. The Berkeley Publishing Group: New York, NY.
[A good introduction to how to assess your real needs, and how to balance self-help, groups, professional therapy, herbals, vitamins, and serious pharmaceuticals.]

Paul, Nina. [2006] Reiki for Dummies. Wiley: Hoboken, NJ.
[The text I use for my Reiki classes.]

Roizen, Michael F., MD and Oz, Mehmet C., MD. (2006) You on a Diet: The Owner's Manual for Waist Management. Free Press, A Division of Simon & Schuster: New York, NY.
[This has a great simple exercise routine in the Appendix. Many depressed people are overweight because the biochem is out of whack, and because we are trying to fill our emotional hunger with high-fat food.]

Shomon, Mary J. (2000) Living Well With Hypothyroidism: What Your Doctor Doesn't Tell You...That You Need to Know. HarperCollins Publishers: New York, NY.
[You can read about hypothyroidism and see if asking for a test makes sense. Some of her assertions are off-base, but she also says things that no one else does, and that everyone needs to hear.]

Simon, Dr. Sidney B. and Simon, Suzanne. (1990) Forgiveness: How to Make Peace with Your Past and Get On With Your Life. Warner Books, Inc.: New York, NY.
[More cerebral and less valuable than the other books on forgiveness, but if you can't face the real work yet, you can read this one and get your courage up.]

Smith, Jean, ed. (1997) Everyday Mind: 366 Reflections on the Buddhist Path. Riverhead Books: New York, NY.
[You don't need to be Buddhist to benefit from these words as you start every day.]

Appendix B:

Meet the Author

Victoria Leo has been coaching people on how to have to live happier and healthier lives for over fifteen years. She has a Master's degree in biological anthropology [think Bones] and graduate Psych education as well as Master/Teacher certification in Reiki energy healing; Life Coaching, with a focus on integrated life/health/career; Clinical Hypnotherapist [this is therapy, not hocus-pocus]; Past Life regression [a wonderful tool for breaking through blockages]; intuitive readings and Chakra Clearing. Victoria has taught in industry, in city and county government, with individuals through her company **Soar With the Eagles**, and at colleges.

Victoria offers a unique blend of techniques and services, focused on exactly what YOU need, not the technique *du jour* or what is trendy. Visit her at www.soaringreiki.com.
If you are interested in her business coaching and career search services, visit www.soarwitheagles.biz. You can also find her and her various books on Facebook, and on LinkedIn. She blogs at http://soarwiththeeagles.wordpress.com but rarely tweets. Victoria's previous book Take Back Your Lost Heart: A Toolkit for Living with Courage and Caring in the Turbulent 21st Century is available on Amazon or through www.lulu.com [print and e-book].

Victoria shares her home in the Pacific Northwest with a herd of cats and rabbits, an engineer who designs new paints and decals for jumbo-jets, and a mobile phone that doesn't do anything except make phone calls.

Soar With the Eagles, POB 9102, Covington WA 98042 www.soaringreiki.com **253.203.6676**

Certificate

Tear out this page and mail to POB 9102, Covington WA 98042 or scan and email to Victoria@soaringreiki.com

** 20% off – or free shipping – on your autographed copy of either Take Back Your Lost Heart or Journey Out of SAD

OR

** 50% off your first Life Coaching, or Intuitive Reading Hypnotherapy session

Call or email and let's determine which gift fits your needs.

This certificate can only be used once per book purchase.

Notes